Bainbridge Island Notebook

Bainbridge Island Notebook

Uche Nduka

ROOF BOOKS
New York

ISBN: 978-0-937804-98-8
Library of Congress Control Number: 2023943275

Cover design by Venn Daniel
Book design by Deborah Thomas
Author photograph by Fiona Gardner

NEW YORK | Council on   This book is made possible, in part, by the New
STATE OF
OPPORTUNITY. | the Arts   York State Council on the Arts with the support
of the Office of the Governor and the New York State Legislature.

Roof Books
are published by Segue Foundation
300 Bowery Fl 2
New York, NY 10012
seguefoundation.com

Roof Books
are distributed by
Small Press Distribution
1341 Seventh Street
Berkeley, CA. 94710-1403
800-869-7553 or spdbooks.org

Bainbridge Island Notebook

They meld
& tingle.
The hemlock
greets
the elm.
Roots grow
brighter.
Wax,
seedlings,
cable.
Symbiosis
or not.
Slick
with nodules
& filaments
we've never
been colorblind
under
constant surveillance.
What you know
everyone knows.

Shoelace
& frame & breath.
Synth line.
Fugue
in between
the sheets.
I never feel
more alive
than when
you're spooning me.
Soft cocoon
& echo of shrubbery.
Rib to rib.
Tattooed feet
as naked as
the music we make.

No one can say
you didn't rock me
till my heart broke
into radiance.
Waiting for lightning
your pleasure
gave me my measure.
The island bit down
hard on garlic
as we rubbed our genitals
on the words
of a song.
We set sail
on softness that
sustained our passages.

I count on the friendship
of robins. Open in flight
in light. To find beauty
in the middle of disaster.
Another way of saying
this is through the lore
of the sails. I hold out
hope for the reappearance
of easeful pining. Moon
on stone sculpture, moon
on boat. Laughing for
no reason on the windowsill
where we're eye to eye
tongue to tongue.

Except by nurture
dark green quotation
marks/

conjunto/ ranchera/ cumbia

life isn't an awful trap

a revival of negotiations
of self-questioning/ self-projection

lonelier since that inner leap

I don't give a damn
about the conquest
of nature

conquer yourself first
(ain't you nature?)

Near the center that
covers uncovers
thighs caresses abysses
we couple without illusions.

Countdown to edgier
                     territory.
Blown into the room
                  by wind:
                          an African headpiece.

We love with flair.
Faces tongues light
                  correspondences of curves.

Errands on the
              threshold of desire.

Wet canvases wet stones
acting out up close
for the first time
in half a shelf space
this tangle of brass & bronze
alternating between talk & silence
various routes into open slopes
a human skull an unframed poster
star power in tatters those
stick figures of meaning
not in the style of an
intruder into enchantment
shadows of afternoons to come
where rains drum on kayak
how does one resist
the dolphins reshaping the coral

Carpool karaoke/

un-
gardened
un-
walled
un-
vipered

just above
the eyebrows
of starlings

love letters
every love
doesn't
have
to be
an accusation

side by side
set
free
from
whispers

A back loading dock.
His cellphone number.
Fishbowl of local news.
Lobby canvas connoisseur.
Surgical masks ballot drop boxes.
Power outages luggage conveyor.
Old barn steamboat pierced navel.
Quicksilver tight swing hard bargain.
Sandstorm tower earwig trinket.
Elevator door brick kiln weather map.
Her cellphone number.
Airbrush clavicle harmonica backflip.
Rainridge towel. Their flirtations
turn into war.

White-hot rage
eye roll logic

not black people
in high places
or black people
blacked out
or targeted
singled out

seven wings
are neighing

you blew your
chance to be
regarded as
something other
than a secret weapon

seven wings are neighing

Still, continuity.
Exploring new realms
of pleasure.
Brook in a tree.
Things go on anyway.
Wet afternoons
of labia & foreskin.
Splendid days ahead
without foggy glasses.
Out of our dug-outs
back forth traveling continually.
The poems think of you
in the Mediterranean light.
Those lips slay me.

He barged into the room
wearing a red cap of hatred.
The offense was deliberate.
Outside: protesters, counterprotesters,
smoke grenades.
I confess I'm not ready to erase
my truths for their comfort.
This is not a rebuke to
the rain bringing back
light. Our lives diverge
but our ideals live in our
bones. He barged into
Congress with the sewerage
of politics. Terror in
the name of the nation.
I'm far from not caring
About April 4, 1968.

Tidal pool
closing in
on halftime.

I go off script.
Placeholders go missing.

There must be more
to the damage
than ink stain on agate.

Loose talk, loose leather.
Questioning myself
on the verge of grace.

This duty to flourish
& go all the way
to the end.

It's not lyric.
It's sorcery.

—What's on the roof?

—Plants

—What are they doing there?

—Talking

—Talking about what?

—Emergency home repairs

—Just that?

—& intersectional lifestyle

—They suck

—May their road be groovy

—Let them try out different roads

—The form of the mind lives under their hats

—Those plants! Those plants!

—A street crossing a street

—Biker bars

As much of this
as I can stand
confusion between static
and eros

as often as
I could boat
ideal form and dizziness
outright

archives burnished
book spines splayed
Scorpio emerging

started to make my move
showed my thirst thought
I was blessed

the ragged flagpole comes
down between the marvelous
and the horrific

the last time I saw you
          you were tearing
the diamond down the last
time I saw you

you were tearing
the diamond down brick
by brick the last time
I saw you

seeking dynamo

or it can take you
to the very edge of chartreuse

how readily you
drag a nasty winter
into your denial of guilt
it's time to tackle
double standards
bigotry swept under the rug
you call it a rapport
I call it sitting up
in bed making cutting remarks
glowering gorgeous sadistic
I didn't know whether
to tell you or not
but anchorites don't interest me
digging in between
those seasons of well-lit raunch

Between the consolation
& the chastisement of
your naked mouth.
The rest is gross error.

Awake to the clarity
of your nudity & symphony of—

prosperity of nudity.

They have schemed against
a captive of rapture.

Ardor for wisdom.

Drunk with crimson
we fully understand what's
happening to us.

Into the silence
a town throws
flesh & bone.

The remotest places
found us easily.

Don't let delight
go unheard.

Feverview.
Brown snowfall.
Purple redress.

Dyke bars.

We're not the ailment
to which we're tied.

Style it.
Score it.
Sign it.

There are no
defects in the seasoning.

Maybe you're here
to change the air
in this room by not sitting pretty.

Silky days of geography in disguise.
Tea spiked with ginger.

He cupped paradise
to his ear.

Offbeat tinkerers.

You drop everything, stakes
lost, dream company, groans.

"Egg salad is still chicken salad
when you think about it."

The bus took its sleepy time
to get to Fish Town.

This living world
& its natural pleasure.

"You're nevering like you never
nevered before."

There's no place apart
I'm unbalanced
                as the unbalanced world

or the heart
                beneath which a cactus waits.

Just for a while
I'm here.
Oblivion is implacable.

But no one can
stop the sky
from walking
into this room now.

& self-punishment
wasn't found in the written
trace of you.

This roadcut, this thicket
this downhill glide
                Into cabin wall.

Air leaned on by a cello.
Hot mess of hard pass.

I'm pierced by your nakedness.
In one we are many.
You bless us who see your face.
I don't care for your overcorrection.
Seeing the three mountains
seemed worth the hangover.

I don't love you less
when the skyscraper
prays.

Satin identifies
                    so much that's true.

Sometimes your lover
is yourself.

This is heavy petting.

The thin line
between reverie & brushfire.

Out of the endless afterthought
the fruit speaks of its own fervor.

I have no wish to be your armor.
Hungering is more important
                    than satiation.

What this bread tells me
                    while I taste its crust.

We wet our hands
in the pantheon of silences.

Old Seattle Window, 1950.

Night skies walk
through the
unsayable.

A light switch
keeps looking for us
and our acoustic
guitars.

We hesitate
to even try to touch
these wildflowers.

Climb that wreck.

From one end of indigo
to another
halving the afternoon.

Longest way home—

between Mozart
and jacaranda
flirtation writes itself.

That crevasse—
ask how it differs
from touching

        your thongs.

❖

As in insistence that survival is jazzy. And there's so much
to closely look at. Searcher and shapeshifting silhouettes.
Don't just read between the lines; read beyond them.
There is something to foretell in curbside composing.

Love falls on the trail in chunks. The true cross of the
foreskin. This rearward ray. Light full of music and lemon-
grass. But they do exist to blaze the amazed. And more is
expected, and more is received. Caresses teach us to see.
They throw pink across silence. Loose strings as well.
Each time we need to decide which pool party to go to.
Stairway with a devolving strobe. It was a privilege to
have brushed wings with you.

Sheer skirt and nylon short shorts. Plant and ankles blur together. A third rustle under a different roof. Lately we did learn of the aria and whims of the rain.

A bootstrap is part of a jigsaw. Cut and blow: it's not a cop-out. But I don't think of it as bedazzlement from start to finish. Where is private equity headed?

Produce posters, prank posters, vandalism after midnight. What a fucking asshole my damn life is. A way of holding onto the initiation of the original friction. Not heavily yet tumbling into eastern lights. The meaning is not in the meaning. There's nothing corrupt about the flesh. My agony can't reduce yours. Eye color, face shape, different channels.

I gather mimosas and Ndebele beads. Finding you, loving you, losing you. For our chance to slip out of the door we must know how much skin music is. 100 miles a second. Board cutters with pieces of a map. Tomorrow's desires and the fight for beauty. A bottle of whiskey in one pocket a poem with a switchblade in another. These pleasures of radiating.

Shadow ripped open by a skeleton. I'm sketching before I walk to the other side of music. To stop giving is to stop living. We need the foliage on drawbridge. Beyond a tight-rope, the seafoam. Acutely aware of the whirl of feral destiny. For inside a digression is the approach of a storm. An adagio asks for nothing now but to shine.

On surfboard in the blizzard. Mild or spicy, observation may vary. Being curious is wrongdoing? Mr. Mango on metered access point. Miss Subway with her feet in the air. As if romance could Protect us from death. Side-saddle, a special kind of terrible. Does brutality see sensitivity? Entirely outside the reality of sweat on your eyebrows. I glimpse you blinding the sunflowers. The gull calls me. In this rite the solar gold is being birthed by darkness.

Even as I travel far from her, Nigeria keeps unsettling
things. Starlight guides me into metamorphosis. I don't
expect tessitura to be bludgeoned by melisma. You
brought the wrong aria while I was putting on my tuxedo.
I think about Brooklyn as it was and think about Brooklyn
as it is. Something must happen to the broken bracelet.

I discovered the musk of a melody. I inhaled it. Main
Street Jefferson and the veiling in figure skating. Simpler to
watch someone look at us sideways where the sidewalk
jigs. Another mouth. Another touch of the wrap. Heaven
drops to one knee. What the songs are chattering about
inside a burning throat. I liked the way our breath fogged
the window.

Look at that desperate flower inside a sword. Next stop
is closer to the edge; the fertility of outsiderdom. A life
rendered coherent by watercolor. The boathouse and its
memory of a glasshouse. Blackouts keep score. I'm yet to
get out of that jam. Chasing a flag that is still frying fish.
The chronicle is about survival, not about a messiah's
panhandle. All in the flow without dilution.

My own time of leave-taking needs a soundtrack. All of me
is in your eyes. Those dances have dreams to remember.
Don't just give me another day; give me another life. A
question scattered among other notions of craft. Ripe for
this hour: parentheses in burgundy. It's been a long time
I've been saying Goodbye. And something far unrulier
to come.

Flying far from half-closed laughter. Outreach mania and
the exact moment you found out how it tastes. When I
play it back in my mind, it becomes relativity. You're not
on a cleanse yet. You sit under an awning and crack jokes
to alleviate the problems of existence. Always fresh, braving
the questions put to you by the world. Around the wrist
and under fingernails.

Maybe that's what it is: a horizontal silence. Think of all
the making and unmaking in a twist. Another tree line,
another rimshot. I hear what you almost say. The alternation
of delight and horror. Singing the city back to the city.
Open palm, starkin. I hope you'll forgive me if I let you
know that I don't like ironic distance.

Something out there is kind to us. Jubilant thoughts speed through tinted windows. But I don't want to ask why you're standing in the shadow of a word. Beyond the stench of vegetable chatter. Elementary wonder makes me uneasy. An instant in haste surrenders to the sun. In the crabgrass I'm saddled with blades to whet. Regrets? I have plenty.

The cracks can't be fully mended. The tip of the tongue whistles what you nearly mean. Those avalanches that govern moments in the sun. A radish shaping up in a hubbub. We fall in and out of harmony. Sketchbook honeysuckle. From the grid to the gut-junk. What do you make of marker and pen on rubies? (Also have them procreate for the big plastic country.)

A snakeskin's doubleheader. What's your favorite song from hell? Civilizing the ether one blast at a time. The state of not understanding may need a new name. Fake eyelashes and tableaux. Meat draped across asphalt. Sadness is fecund. This is the way it is: there are knives inside your language. I'm bored with distanced boredom. I hate sleeping without you.

I wanted to make a shape of a certain pleasure. Slow excavations of desire. The stem of a flower and the other half of Midtown. We're mythological creatures. There is a sense of freshness in our biology. What's going on? Has self-sabotage gone out of fashion? A way to hear the light and become lettuce. During which you uncrossed your legs.

Midwinter hasn't made any progress. Solitude is entangling. The night throbs, haloed with semen. Clouds played a role in the formation of your light. Destiny is in disarray. Nose strip and earband. But the labyrinth is our birthright. The footage remains inconclusive as it should. Don't turn me into a cold marble statue. Darkness isn't sure of us anymore.

Your words enrich the soil. Among the noons farther up our thighs and butts. We're creatures that distances cannot fathom. Lace in space and notation. I want to find out the questions still hiding inside answers. Re-prosed as demolition/dissension. Between what is and what is voiced. There's a sudden plunge into merriment.

Wowed into purple rinse and carotene lipstick by the
bottle-blonde. She is a fabulous crisis. The good weather
gathers evidence for the prosecution. A prettified version of
an ugly country. It's a stance taken too far. Their one-and-
only contrivance. Guttersnipes did make it into the filmic
record. In steel-studded gloves, Death became a reliable
roadie. Slick creeps in sleaze-soaked warzone connect.
Pursuing paranormal pleasure by the train tracks.

There is a flipside to fine tuning. Our walk getting under-
way. Taking down the effigy. At Stony Hill they stoned him
to death. Mikey. They stoned Mikey to death in Jamaica.
The stampede in burning markets. Allegiances in counter-
poise. What were they expecting? Not a space of space but
extortion of lost connections. Now beauty is an argument
on a street corner. There's a war between a flag and an
olive branch. Doves are due for re-enchantment.

Honeycombs in a mangrove. Flotsam in the mirror. The
amplitude of a drowning piano. So far, so crazily good.
The dust moves with its own twist. This staircase of talis-
manic craving. No telling what he might do in the woods
by a creek. Salvage the seventh sense. She is a guide in her
own right and in her own light. We didn't come from
nothingness. We have everything. Pilgrims on the trail
of exquisite love.

The space between words and a reader is not empty. Past the living room a blue flame follows a long black overcoat. We'd do well not to bother with cleverness. The hold of that country over you hasn't loosened. I might as well talk to this pork pie. You could see nothing around you but the screen. Shaking the gates of heaven. I might as well speak to this pork pie about the significance of houseplants. Disorder behind the order. Entrance is in the rear and they're turning out elegant essays about a rough text. The higher we climbed the less we saw. Something must be done to maintain disequilibrium.

I'm among the few nuts loose in the planet and I don't want you to love me to death. Spill the wine on pagecraft. There's no one home to hustle pistols and phalluses. I get to keep your lost things. A drinking song is becoming our national anthem. I've been an enemy of the state since birth. Check out the winning flag sometime. Certainty begins to resemble a gamble. I throw ten mistakes in the air to get to a surplus. This doesn't explain the gray in actuality. Digression is holy. Can't split distraction from attention. The traffic light changed. My heart skipped a beat.

Pleasure isn't the only source of the erotic. More rocking, less talking. The life and lies of a walker on the High Line. Don't ghost an almost American man. I bow before kind lovers and their telepathic velocities. Until you hear what the wind is saying you'll never be free. Disturb the dreams of the executioners. A hard look routs indifference.

Empty the garbage can, water the lilies. Magnolia on her breath. The invisibility of light. Almost brown swallowing you whole. The pressure on the petunias. Thy will is dissonance. Pacific ecstasy. The sexual skylight in the soundtrack that is playing. Why is justice mostly deferred? The crops are failing. You skip from taxi to taxi. Days surge and combust. And then childhood reopens. And thus, taxidermy is thrown up. As soon as the cannonade appears, you sail further into the self. I feel deeply suspicious of your claim to have understood my solitude. This afternoon must respect the act of peeling tomatoes or else...

There are times I let the sun wash my hair and let minerals scream. The combustions want out. The aquarium catches fever. Adrenaline rises and falls from the hermaphrodite. Powerfield of disequilibrium. Out of a belief in silhouette, let the latitudes somersault. My crisis tears geography apart. There are stones between sighs. I'm sorry it has come to this terrible innocence deep in the seasickness of a cathedral. Loves glow through you but birds fly into my hands. We're transformed beyond recognition.

Break through the fiberglass and get to the jellyfish. Ribcage, ripcord. The friction, the shadings. Listening is the act of shining although there's something to the baseline of peril. Your spine proclaims something about marsh-light and you declare that you're not puny. Transition is available in the levitation of meows. You know the power of shitty mornings. To hold it close but not to erect it. Damn the rain. An amalgam of fiddlehead and hammer.

What got us here wasn't the deliberate suppression of science fiction. There was the mystery of flesh inside flesh in the baths. That love went beyond the imagination and registered how we felt about elixir. Each sentence knocked against a showerhead. We were there to have a good time. Lay with language three or four times inside the wound. We developed new methods of changing the bedding. Your workarounds made me feel less alone. More to the point, we rolled a rain barrel into the street.

It doesn't have to hurt for it to be love. Whatever must they have made of me in those days? Love says Uncross your hands Uncross your legs. My body your body turning the world upside down. And there's no better way to live our love to the fullest. Your body my body turning the light inside out. The curvatures we inhabit, the parabolas... Our past: off the wall. Our past: down under. That foul-mouthed hypercritical eye. We decide from a distance what to do with a faded sign. Come close to the crater.

Was to make me wish I was not desperate to get out. You're either someone who likes wearing shorts or someone who doesn't. Plain speaking is overrated. The dream of riding a bicycle forever. An act of desperation in many different circumstances. I stop paying attention because from the first clarification I'm bored out of my mind. Handlebar mustaches, scotch and soda. I plan to die with my boots on. Hold on to your love handle.

Gestures of cool cast shadows. Nightclub is a language. Pheromone and caramel fill a vacuum. You stick your fingers in your ears and wonder what the hell is going on. It's everything at once. There's vitality in joy. Each framework falls apart and it's deeply personal. Absolution triggers a slight alarm. I don't have to shout to show you I'm an eviscerator of speedy lock and key and toasty wardrobe. Thanks for talking me up the ladder! To give and give tongue.

Sitting in the center of your perception. Compassion over murder. I offer that energy back to you. The doorway stays open depending on how you reach out. I had a long week. My energy is going off the charts. I freely admit I'm a limelighter. Logic wrestles with me. I shred quietude. I assume the ragged poet glory. I don't run around looking for drum-splattered words. If you pay attention to the growl, it grows much louder. I walk alone with a cruel souvenir.

Postcards from the seaside. You got a kick out of the fetish stuff. The nerve! Being in the way of the sun that decided to shine on ruins. Go find somebody who is a better fit than me. Reset your threat. If I wanted to, I could be petty about that kind of shit. I don't want you to project that darkness on me. You can disconnect. Hearing you say that is like staring into the eye of a hurricane. You're only as good as the whip in your hand. Strumming into a winged scarab.

If you've been touched deeper than you've ever been touched before. Alternating between comfort and tension. Some people choose to live like that. Awesome and scary, I don't know what to do with this power. My physicality is very delicate. Sleeping bag, plastic straw, plastic hangar. Commuter moments threaten the shipment of reveries. We've never wanted anything. You and I are fire hazards.

So much is happening here if you know where to look. New ways to love beyond design interventions. The paroxysms of depth. The terror of that kiss. I'm going to rob the day of its acid reflux. You don't need special eyes to see a body that clenches, that twirls. I'm at liberty to speak on these things. All of them. The sentences press on my nerves. Moderation doesn't come naturally to me. It feels right to attune to the vibration of your lust right now. The bliss that vibrates in your note. You are who you are as you slip into your upper truth. Light entering light. Is this the experience you wish to call into your life? One for each hand: level 12 chaos. At this moment the afternoon is enough. Lover going into lover.

We don't know how we came here or why. We don't know ourselves or why we can't live together. I'm not trying to follow you to the end of the road. There's no time to live your razzle dazzle. I put my hand inside a stony noon. I'm not trying to calm the rough waters. I tend to find sorrow clean. Downwind is the right direction. The sandy beach is boring me to death. I've been giving you my less troubling news. The blanket has got something to say to a red rain. In the corner, my hands leap to write.

If you don't hear this, you won't get to know how to love with pen in hand. A disorder wraps this up. A light that wanders noisily and hits the floor. I've libeled the trees as much as I could. I've cut out the bleeding. There's more. Always with you there's more. A lexicon of horror in the cracks of a conversation. Beverage co-pay; rubber band foot-noted. Something about surfacing resentment even though it's supposed to be over. I can smell the low tide of burning coals. I can't bear to give up a blank page. Disturbances from an elevator landing. The sky doesn't see anything but us. Gazing through the hill of bones there's a warning about the wind becoming claws. The last time we checked he was facing the right way. High on mushrooms and Vivaldi, he couldn't dream of ringing a better bell.

Left the symbolic side of a broken water pitcher. Chain of molecules in the cracks of clues. Another night with streamside candy ball. And you mapped my body with your soul. And the fruit got juicier as we lay. Try to play this on a drum. Beating a dead horse becomes necessary for a while.

What mattered, in any case, was that they did everything to be of service in that junta-ruled country. Connivance made them mediocre. Moral evasion was seldom shaken. They never grew wise to the shifting shape of constraint. Because the situation hasn't changed. Because he is still writing with a paddle. And there's time to get back on your feet again. Not saying you have much regard for safety. Quicker than swimming to the other side.

Bite the hand that frisks us? Is this vision of actuality worthy of us? I could hear the bus chugging before it became visible. Before the grill, you've got to marinate it the right way. And the pretty girl returned as an old woman to a waiting bowl of freesia. In flight we entwine in the light. No sidestepping of success as a fugitive concept. Ganja time in airport light. Shred the skid and start again under the umbrella of the cum. There are better things to do than failing to fail. This shining obliquity of a peculiar angle. I aim to revalue the uglier feelings of a conjuror. The tweaking of negative theory. Nights lit up by nausea. Novelty is assumed to be oppositional. I don't agree with that assumption. The hour pulls you into your coming obsession.

It's not because you're feeling generous with mere lust that
I submit to the territorial imperative of your juice. How
you invest the licking is up to you. Even in New York, I
long for New York. I'd rather sing, but I don't know how.
Being dragged into the middle of pageantry. I try to photo-
graph the air. A junction into which I splashed black
paint. I'm no longer a spring chicken and must dutifully
acquire reading glasses. I fail at accepting awful things as
normal. In trouble, I've been in trouble for not always
letting the spirit outpace the flesh. A skeleton with a book
growing out of it. To confound unfreedom, to rout it.
Yearning for gazebos, she is more than a poet in the mall.
Searing the loom, the motherlode, her fury is everlasting.

I find this awfulness asinine. I bow to the crest of shadows.
Backstreet wheat. I won't survive without all my losses.
Let's surf on the goofy stuff together. The nature of things
doesn't give a damn about our natural selves. Daily food
still gets cooked. A melancholy through which an island
comes alive. We came at uncoinciding times in our prone
positions. Don't underrate him. His idiocy is lethal. Some-
one has sailed to Bainbridge Island, a benison, in less
obvious ways life isn't all bad news, he owes huge debts
to relocations, all over what's deeper than the places that
fall into him, not all gaps need to be bridged, those
unwatched hours of forming thoughts matter to someone.
Ride me back to not giving a shit, this is the practice of
the unfinished, the bedding far from our feet our hands,
the days perfecting our looming graves, to be truly foreign
to something, to someone.

As would our ancestors who knew the genre of this movie.
What is this love? What will this love be without hair
dryers? Into seaweed. Into stalactites. Into mementos. Not
routine in graphite. One line. Two lines. Black love storm.
Less watching, more rocking. Bamboo. Hot red metal box.
Those toenails, those cocktails. We should have done this
earlier. We need to acknowledge and face things we don't
understand. As if impaled on a poem. To tell the truth of
the city moving as if to music. Glazed with inherited
grievances, radioactive dust included. The deep sea within
a train whistle. Or the right measure. Which right measure?
The place of revolutionary consciousness. Despite the
stories of our love in ancient texts. Hang the posters.
Shovel the snow. Sweep the floor. Cut the lawns. Deliver
the soup. From our first sip to our last trip. We walk past
the wishing lanterns, the champagne glasses on wet grass.

Believe me when I say hysteria is precious. The providence
of disillusionment. Talking about the fretless bass that
breaks every barrier. The rebuke of bloodstains in Kharkiv.
How long did it take to discover that perfection is lethal?
Goodbye, goodbye. Who has offended the ash-heap? She
was chased into the sea to drown. Dialectical inversion in
drone cameras. Do away with torture. Do away with track-
ing shots. I'd rather not get hung up on the crosscutting
between mercury and pasture.

To comprehend the underlight. What the connection was or the reverse. This is a strong argument for your own way of formatting. Put your name somewhere and then you won't care as much. Not the stuff that was in the newspaper three days ago. Your portion. Beyond headlines where the shape of liberation shimmers. That type of conspiracy becoming common place. The evidence of what you anticipate. Discussable as timbral resonance. Anti-expertise. Anti-mastery. As they deflect and distract. No fingerprints on purple heritage. Getting lost in the crowd, sensitive to wind from the north. Beauty is the shelter, and the shelter is vulnerable. To tap into a sex unseen behind the seen. Your voice, your life.

Crab stew, bucket, mops. Why do you want your meanness to be heroic? Is it better to crack up than to laugh? The racket of the attic is such a steal. Checked pants, digressions full of anthems, a fistful of peanuts. Eyebrow raising soapstone, brownish light, insomniacs. A new old wound, a text on a quest, whoever approaches the shadow on the lagoon of the alphabet. It's possible to pay too little attention to the marvels of hieroglyph, to overlook the clothes that fall across a marble floor. The poetry of the butthole is not an effortless trespass.

❊

Looking for a mind spread out on the rug, maybe.
I don't see you anymore. Where have you been?

I'm saving all my money. I've spent too much here.
I want them to know that I didn't take it lightly.
I didn't want to be with someone who didn't want to
  be with me.
They wish to dilute the horrors of the genocide
  in Biafra.
In good faith I will turn you on to those who turned
  me on.

If you kept a record of ecstasies or combat drones, gun-
sight footage.

The rainmakers that read
the old notebooks thought
they were over the top they
thought they knew what they were
getting themselves into there ought
to be tougher liquid feel to them
a different profile emerges when
you turn the bottles around
exciting things do happen they move
boundaries for us the more you think
about them the more useful they
become a different type of sweetness
the same thing happens when the
presence of chlorophyll is quite deliberate

That time when
green lotus
bifurcated brainbirds. Our undies took
the damp grass for granted.
Being present in the
body is necessary while
entering paradise.
Bowing deeply
toward the south
the south

         the south.

Alphabets of clouds.
       Incarnations in the rough.
This happiness is particular
     & crucial.
The baroque can't compete
     With this moment.
I say Love & like it.

Sometimes I shut
my mouth, said
Language.

Caresses in dialogue
bloom all day.

Notice how we're
saved from
pacific ruin.

Impersonality is
an empty socket.

We don't see
& cannot know
what is between
interval & completion.

Angle of sun
on pubes

self-sown bedsheet
black crosses
of Coptic stitch

another way
of being
in the tongue-weave

& that's true
of love
in its starkness

an afternoon with you,
at least in murmuration

Their gospel
is racism
with a beer gut.

Bagel on dirt.

The jabbering.
The shenanigans.

The whack the knack
you don't have to wait
for tomorrow
to rock & roll

the love thereof

how can I accept
their romanticizing
of the ghetto anymore

or the stab
of time gaps

I actually sleep
with the ineffable

if dancing is
a sanctuary
why do you dread it

When the Goddess wants to write
she uses me.

Her ensemble gives me the chills
gives me the thirst
for milk & dew.

In each line that drags me along
I build her a shrine.

Like when the poem becomes
a golden harmonica
& Impressionist painting.

Living?
Do it for a lark, not in
deadly earnestness.

I shiver on her door I drown
In her map.

In other rooms—
the flashing of half-mad
black orchid what I know now
a crack in mimesis
the things a fifth
turning carried

I don't want
to be American poetry's
best kept secret

but enough about us
a name isn't everything

virginity rocks

I hug you
I hug an approaching
carnival

a darkness
that is echoed
so often that it becomes
a light

the coastline
points out our obsession
with softness

heading north
we lull the fog
into believing in us

naked we move
toward the bed
a milestone glimmers

The alley of wisdom
is the alley
         of wandering pines

Your hypochondria
         is their hypochondria

Moonstone   wordstruck

In this harried epidermis
the dead can still
help us

chronicle life's
         frenetic swerves

use the next door
to enter madness

Her western review
on Winslow Way.

Longboard,
amber, pacific rain.

The dude abides.

That's going to make
for a good movie shot.

Topsoil.
Taste of stone.
Cry of plant.

It happened
at the Combahee River.
She positioned freedom
Right there.

Don't talk about rearranging things
It's brutal it's blurry
I relearn the code of the wind
when it circles me & the island
Neither remembers partition or ease
I used to worry about this kind
of thing it may seem grandiose
but I'm not stuck in a rut don't
talk about stopping the beautiful
internal discourse of sexual
intercourse Spanish moss cuddle
lipstick eyeliner my entire life
has been leading toward this

All evening
between land & water
my wife strolls
through the island
wearing her bohemian beret
she officiates over
intensities of music
                    & serenity

her hands merge
            with the free breath
                        of pulp of fruit

her harmonics perennial
                  in errant vowels

After having an oat milk latte
I wandered around the Black
Forest with Trakl & Holderlin &
Rilke. Primers of bloodlight. A close
reading of a portion of the rain.
Drift of dusk inside my task. Glimpses
of this city built upon a clit. Wanting
to touch you at the critical moment
of migration. Wanting to survive
the lash of the ash. They exact
revenge, carry bags of thank-yous.

Boatbuilder afloat.

                His spell.

What the skin breeds
where our glowing ends.

                Her spell.

May your body
always be filled
with the love
you fill my body with.

Beetling syntax

                Of birdsong.

Desire sublimed into rapture.
These truths of waist beads.

Our questions put to a pout
at certain hours.

When she comes
to a place of
no hesitation
& blown kisses
It all adds up.

Do you use
the greater love
to expel the lesser?

A core of devotion
from first to last
as I fall apart
in your arms.

I don't like snow
that has anything to prove.

You don't have to start
from the scratch with
bad air quality everybody
is trying to figure it out
swings shift of static
alongside surfacing to
sway dreadlocks to clicks
markings fucking exhausted by new wreck

Violators will be towed
while I read your bread.

Paging Christopher Okigbo
before they close the barn door.

With gauche paints
you did it/
it was all you.

An advance team
ran his bus off the road.

Scorched the limits.
They accused each other
of othering the other.

Showered calendared deliberate shaming.
Piled catastrophe upon catastrophe.

Gourd of gold. Panther guardian.

The legibility of mortality
Is always multiple.

& I think of loam & morning
& depression.

This weather is not different
from the news. This embrace
is not different from memory.

Bitterness is a hell of a drug.
Nitrous city aquiver with full disclosure.

Solar cascade.
That part where
those yet to be born

drag their secret faces out of secret drawers.

You & the buzzard
were one & did
not belabor the dedication
to craft

not crotch-counting but
the texture of sex

& what if a poem is
a room that has been
wildly lived in

block by block fugues gnaw
at a wet street

what, then, remains to be done
in this felicitous
& beautiful darkness

bring the hula
bring the circus

Don't look for good teakettles
in this vacation park. Everything's
not fine.

With odometers
rolling back before a crabcrawl.

Talk about a more tearable plastic
sponge. River cruise, shooting range.

If ice is a variant of marble
am I defining myself in opposition
to you?

Penalized by paradise
as we ride in this open car
each instance of roughness
exposed to the sun.

Most Nazis went
to Argentina to hide
after World War 2.

The perfect country
for racial hatred
& the Tango stolen
from African slaves.

I'm anxious
& a bookbag is burning.

Why keep tripping on yourself?

The screw-up moves through time.

Like it should
Monday distils   a syncopated coda

weight of the world   half-spoken

I don't know
the answers
& I'm not
even sure what
the questions are

these laws make little sense

now I've got to the door
but I'm yet to earn
sweetness & light

Barricades inside a spell.

What is a wet day
but a tongue
inside an asshole.

Mixing up the hills
& hexes.

Another view
of half the sky.

Point from which
Code Red enters.

The groundwork of speaking
to the sea.

That winning touchdown.

Do I objectify myself?
Yes, I objectify myself.
I'm on top of things.

Bigfoot, cookbook
& colloquial cool.

Southward:
a revivifying look
at the island.

Stalemate cross-marked
with contagious sanctity.

Din of breakage.
Oldest member of the family.

No, not a skyline... semblance of bitten light.

Cup for two
a poem to wake up the dead.

Bless up, Sista.
Blessup.

Loses himself in the summer
of your hair.

In the summer inside your hair.

You're the daughter of the ocean
& the sun loves your rebellion.

Bless up, Sista.
Blessup.

Loses himself in your intrigue
& sleeps in front of your door.

Come home, Carlota Lukumi.

Who needs to hear another
bloody poet nattering about
another tree

the skies that have strolled
with me
know my language

I draw the poem
I don't puzzle through it

Due in no small part
to the fact that these
choruses are good
at saying No

I can't proclaim
love loudly
& then withdraw

Feel the alarm
that justifies
the accent of disgust

I'm spending
a whole day waiting
until a phrase
delivers the requisite turmoil

Better be good
to the snare drum

Sliding up
into the dark interior
of your thighs

The voices of all the flowers
a garden knows

Flute-note
redoubled above your breasts

Smoke joints
play revolutionary songs
at my funeral.

I may need to shower
alongside the Secretary
of Desire & the
Minister of Anxiety.

Teetering between
a miniature portrait
& a difference of
opinion once we're
out of earshot.

Come on raffia!
Come on cowries!

That footage is creepy.
Has anyone in Lagos
Seen my car keys.

A way to let things go
to just let them go & not
to continue trying to explain
myself to myself I haven't had
the need to reinvent the senses
in a way vinegar is also involved
I'm done with playing my cards
close to my chest we're hardwired
from birth to taste the light it can
turn your truth your wound around
this love that is already within us
all around us every connection becomes
a chance to really taste your coffee
how did happiness get to be so distorted

Considering the velocity
of songs.

A storm around a finished
& unfinished thought.

An invisibility to be destroyed.

Rousing the Talking Drum.
Self-surveillance in the groves
                          of Oshogbo.

An invisibility to be cross-pollinated.

                    More intensity
                          to the nanosecond.

Another rainbow staggering out of the ocean.

When it comes down
to it
I'm committed to making
an unholy racket

a knee rip says yes
a crotch rip says
absolutely yes

this has much to do
with assegai
Italian terrazzo stonework

becoming more relaxed
about the feast
above the belly button

there's almost no place
you can't be in a
catcher's crouch

& sooner or later
moving into & out
of each other

the rough waters
                do leave something behind

polish is a phantom

it's not a hard pause

when love nails us
to a hammock

fog shows us the impossibility
of possession

depth calls for the mixing
of registers

Didn't give a shit anymore
about carbon footprint

heck, that was said
in cold blood

the hitchhike is restless
& unappeasable

how to face the tamarind
effect how to face the black
table talk

this needs to be an
orchestra (unless I missed something
& it already is)

passing through a rock pool

in the book's tide
& bottlegourd

there are no recession
worries
during Trooping the Color

too late in the day
to develop
a genetic quirk

they are still being

killed by shelling

several dolphins waiting
to run out the clock

Other things are happening
on the balcony   their private
fantasies are brilliant   with
afternoons I'm a different sort
of lover   two skies &
red-hot fauna become conjectural

we angle our torsos
into the shadow   must be
the music we've been
playing   an ecstasy that
is perennial   like the
necessity of intimacy   it couldn't
have been said better
on a falsetto   another use for
Take one   Take two   Take three
every news is in the profile   inside the
shadow
                    dehiscence put to use in interludes

Debunking the difficulty
of belief

how luxe is
your sailboat's hull

(sartorial daring
be damned)

harmonies
superfluous harmonies

the inescapable faith
of hyphens

someone's gotta pay
for self-corrections

in addition
to the reach of motive

I quote lines
from my favorite
movies & success becomes
an attitude until I destroy
myself again

& that's because
we're all hiding under
ironic distance

seeing the crease
between prayer
& sayer

silverpoint in which
certain alphabets
might explode

How little I knew

it was booed into
the ground because
it was making too
much sense

love you till Friday

poetry isn't walking
all over everybody
you can't convince me
that it is
what do we do now
I have no intention of
writing anything timey
I don't know whether
this is where it's at
why bother if you're not
going to astound

I expect to be misinterpreted
for buying my own groceries

always crashing
in the same couch

pull down the blinds
my reaction
to certain saxophones

very simpatico
crying with laughter

I'm the wrong way round
on the onbeat

fracture a reaction

I didn't stop the world
& get off
as you suggested

all the way through
sucked right into the center of it

you don't belong
to me I don't belong to
you we're here to serve
the servant

Eyesight to the overture
the fiddle about
keyhole

beyond the candles
I venture back
to your lips

subjectivity is fragrant

seeing what's in my head
my feelings ain't waiting
around to be clarified

I hammered the hell out
of that poem & thought
Is that where I am now

a dry mix a left-handed screw

glad I got to see you
most of the time

I fell into a gap
& came across a photo
of you & decided not
to stick with what works
for me

a nod to the transparency
of giant bronze
arachnids

wherever pavilions take you

always something about
a rock goddess I can't think about
anything else

take a dip
but keep the fire lit

are you worried about
the tyranny
of measurable results

& here I am
laughing & trying
to wrap my head
around this country
that allows me to speak
of myself in the third person

                    light at a certain height

                              gives thanks you're alive
As the cynics watch
your middle age
becomes a work of art

the street
gives a toast
at the wedding of two gardens

you're a triple taurus

the poem needs a new hat

things are alright
but slower

this ferry goes to Manhattan

I feed myself
so that my poems
won't starve

this is a Nobody
who is actually a Somebody

One wrong move
& the momentum
would be lost but here's
where to sow a text
with a salty finish it's
part of the road you
need to travel in each
other's arms flavors open
up in a different way
in endless arousal (another
bloom, another heartbeat)
off-notes you can dive in
& out of

tip-top-tap
wineglasses between
your toes

Being in tune
when I touch your
knees your shoulders
you peel me back
to vibrant purity
the fully dressed
poems & the naked
ones are looking for
each other you let a
few lines lead us
to magic

Sliding past
yesterday's bread

looking up
at the stars
between skyscrapers

a taste
of what's to come

spiral metal
Ferris wheel
prayer shawl

it isn't me
writing
it's the pilot light

this shadow is my own

I didn't think
I was measuring
my anticipation I
didn't think about
that at all

where?

see you in print

then he was born

between love
& loneliness

against scrutinized dispersals
the candor of uninterpretable
buildings

split kiss by kiss

Compromise caught by
the waist. Our greenings,
like emergencies. Those
serigraphs; an eclogue
northgating. Have some
patties or something!

When he throws himself
into a book I thumb my
nose at him.

He has a buzzword
for the crisis of our age.
It's better than disinvestiture.
The prevailing rhetoric
or the signature of indifference.

Why are you so restless?
You can't put a cap on it.
They can't play us until they play us.

There's nothing impermissible
in the bunker.

What's the value of this blueprint?

Something quite other than
god-awful rumor,
guns trained on their backs.

That nullity spoke to me
but that wasn't where
I wanted to live.

I grab a table lamp,
unroll a paper towel.
Transience bleeds into
palmwine.

The suntanned professor
always thought
you have no right
to love yourself this much.

& then there's the fact
that you cherish
your helplessness.

Into the wound.

The thickening ignition
is unnerving. Things ain't
looking up.

I took a vow of volubility.

Because
you stopped for a word with me.
Because
you stopped for a word with me.

Among the bathers
purity of intent
is plainly tedious.

The solid ground waits
only for those that sleepwalk.

The rain dons a skimpy lingerie.

Oblongs are great
if you're on the inside.

I slip through the slot
of masonry.

& red excursion
beckons

but the hour
must be cleared of stones.

The oar sways
left & right.

I row to the mouth
of the river.

The 40 acres & a mule
never materialized. (Another
broken promise.)

Gaslit.

I'm the country he abandoned.

When will the long
war end?

& the canyon splinters.

It's not yet time to move
into the rafter.

We're stumbling flawed beings.

You lie across the fretboard,
I always loved your
ear-wear,
the bough whose canaries
are stanzas,
don't come to me
if you think I'm done,
wherever you may be
with the endless voice
of the lover calling
the beloved, my eyes hurt from
watching the moving
legs of trees,
it's not with ease
that I step into my final years
but I still want to smell you.

As an emissary of darker light
I take it as a compliment when
someone steals one of my books
from a bookstore.

The tracery of buttoned egg.
The rockslide rides
to a still point.

Philosophy isn't value neutral.
That is, in the very act of love.
Being altered going forward & backward.

I'm a permanent muse.
I'm of some use.

There's no such thing
as a nation
without bloody hands.

How to fully
square all that or not.
I've got a project for you.

With you
between you & you.

Full hair, full chair covers
twisted by
the full weight of contention.

Too much for anyone
who won't let the raiment
of light fall away.

Your story won't make sense
without conflictions.

Telling it not
& telling it hot.

As I collide with your face
as I collide with your startext.

I had been on a tear.
I held nothing back.

I stood so close
          to the balladry of beauty.

That infinity
          between your open legs.

Scribbling like mad
                    across a tower hiding
                              from a lightning bolt.

I had spoken to you about
                    the bedrock of divine intelligence.

Old sambas. Wole Soyinka's afro.

In you each of us
finds something of ourselves.

In foreskin's point of view
the music sought me out.
I can pull anything out of
my hat even when I'm in the
grip of a tropical smoothie.
Pain nets me joy nets me.
I trouble the brambles often.

She
parts
her
hair,
parts
her
lips,
slips
from
one
ecstasy
to
another.

When we gather
in the gash
& pull the arrow
out of each other.

I live between your
stanzas. My thighs
are open to your
open secret. Door
upon door, I don't
mean to deceive you
with a freshening. Fluted
desire imposes a turning
point on us. Naked
beside the arch. I
see you in the best light.
The last thing the sky sees
is your distaste for moderation.
Off the track. Off the cuff.
You & I merging
                    into a single stem.

Not knowing how to pray to you
trying my best to pray to you.

Primestar freshens the chimney.
A name in black letters.

                         Whatever
does not recur is suspect.

Skylighting as we cut logs.

We hold hands & make old worlds
new again.

Staring at an abattoir.
Staring at a cradle.

Riding on a horse
between tombstones.

I didn't know anything
in the split second before
                        the roast.

Like when diplomats become hustlers.
Like listening to a dreaming denim.
Otherwise choose who you want to
be on the other side of this anxiety.

Artillery keeps shattering.
Our nipples shine through the streets.

On a good day here, someone is dying
in a war somewhere.

A crack on a wall is an orchid.

Why put off till tomorrow
the fun you can have today?

You drew a line
between the moon & me.

I'm back to watching screwball comedies.

The flesh remembers her bounty.
Love can't be stripped of ellipses.

Get rid of space.
Get rid of the guidebook.
Don't look this up
on the internet.

The revolution is always beginning.
Pessimism is cheap.

Assault
Murder
Hatred
Injustice
Intimidation
have not become old news.

Each time you come around.
Each time you come ambling down.
Each time you come tumbling down.

An exit from
the I leads to
            an entrance into
                        the I.

My anger is not for sale.

God stood to the side, smiling.
He was fittingly rumpled.

The mantra radiated color.
The light wore a brown robe.
Wake me when my silence
gets uncomfortable.

I'm not deaf
to the music
of
your
eyes

Where were we
supposed to make love
if
not
between
the
church
pews

A penumbra
decodes our secret oath,
danger on
the sidewalk.

If to love is to travel
let this be a journey.

The book chose
to land on
my head in a pandemic.

I've remembered a lot
& forgotten a lot. Boats

& ambulances pass by
as I lick salt
off your breasts.

Dipped a feather
into Puget Sound.

Downwards
to a feasting boy,
kernel oil,
camwood.

Poetry sprouts on
            a trail.

Destemmed grapes
            find concrete.

Sweet beginning
            of a bitter end.

It needn't always be
            us against the world.

That's just the way
            it is with my sensorial
                  understanding of this place.

Democracy is a disguise
            in itself

in the edifice of routine
      or those structures of taste
            in a glass of seawater.

But somehow, I got through
the pauses in crisis.

Close to grassblue roaming free.

Gardens without a gardener.

How the war changed
the way the Igbo understood
themselves.

Going faster with hot steppers.

Horrors you can prepare for.

Fragments adorned in scars.

Leave that bit
(like that) as bitter as
it is   no one can totally
avoid what's unreasonable
something going on right
in front of you that you
shouldn't miss   so think about
going big even when you're
wearing elbow patches

                    not that you give offense
                    to canna lilies
                    when you're talking nonsense
Leave that bit
     (like that) about the Scarecrow
     & the fallen field marshals

Those stories
that ferried us
across the diaspora

for the oar the anchor
the toast is always
open

inside looking out
to the lush feelings
of this landscape

I carry my cities
around with me

the weather
the season
last night's attack on us

I didn't fling words
around with abandon

neither did you

At Canyon de Chelly
At Little Big Horn
At Sand Creek

In Salem

At Nagasaki
At Hiroshima

Such as it is— civilization
such as it is— wilderness.

A leveling out, a benediction.

But I'm not known
for keeping an even keel.

Don't get hooked
on the blinding speed
with which urns multiply.

Did Gauguin explain
the explainer while painting
island life?

*

One round of charades.
Tupperware, scaffold shed.
Nightstand notepad.
Dancing in the wings.
A flight to board.
Those I've wronged.
Available ticket for a concert.
Licking her lips.
A busy day ahead of monochromatica.
Redemption reckoning.
Cheetos & beer.
To make amends.
Rehearsal franchise.
I'm already devastated.
Meals on wheels.
Contract details.
Bodega carnations.
I can't do it alone.
Pot of caviar & red gingham.
A big budget romcom.
Rocking back & forth in thought.
Evergreen branches.
Lots of dark makeup under my eyes.
His mortal coil.
Vamping in the Intro.
I'm the spirit of the season.
Via their voicemail.
Polish off the leftovers.
One gifting spot.

A melting champagne bottle.
I'm not free of judgment.
A set of prawn placemats.
Merci beaucoup!
One of my don'ts became a do.
Canvas: tablescape.
Splurge on sour cream.
Centerpieces of high & low.
Sheetmetal, fostering new friendships.
I simply insist on not making it fancy.
Edelweiss is their theme.

Alewife, unblinking obstinate symmetry.

Cursive on shrimp cocktails.

Bed-Stuy living room I think of often.

A hard hitter, not a phoned-in answer.

Who's never said No to being profiled?

A poor handshake is not necessarily a blunder.

To get into a canoe.

I distrust constant serenity.

Having a very hard time with her first spoken line.

Don't force your guests to mingle.

You're not getting enough of the details.

Fingers on the strings.

A turnaround in alignment, in pomegranates.

Let the shit out. Go to the deep end of the pool.

How are you responding to the wedding I bring
    to the table.

Those things teaching us to say them.

How the spirit has the audacity to be raunchy
    is wonderful.

This is not the outsider's gaze.

Solitude that started before quarantine.

A contentious debate is necessary.

Wait for a straw hat.

A familiar pettiness is being meted out.

The desert adds a thought here.

I was confused about the heartbreak that took root.

That flight of birds inside a drumroll.

Because of her, by way of her, in a red raincoat.

I salute you, Impermanence.

There were immigrants then. There are immigrants now.

It's a throw of the dice. Right now, they are killing Asians in the streets of America.

If I'm not back in 5 minutes, wait longer.

Compassion without knowledge is empty.

Who is boycotting whom? I'm ready to melt into
   red maple leaves.

The subterraneans aren't interested in context.

I get hopelessly lost in hard blues.

Even inside a house of reeds, you've got to take the heat.

There's no wrong way to cry.

They lie to you when they tell you that you have only one
   life to live.

Back to what was an FBI break-in.

Let's play find-the-pepper. Is there lucidity after Biafra?

The brook questioning the lake.

It's never too early to live the unlived.

When will the colonizing stop?

Poetry against misery.

We're going to get up in the morning to one
   commonality: richness.

My purpose is not on the clock. It goes beyond time.

You're more than that pain.

Sun Ra treated us rather kindly.

The lovers unhoused by the Atlantic of her will.

A willingness to make space & hold space for complexity.

Nothing prepares you for drowning in bills.

Different things will pop out of a travesty.

This is their play. A scuffle during the breach.

Los Angeles is where you go to forget history,
   erase history.

A passport linked to mushrooms.

The satire that defies desire. Do you smell the fumes?

At least you can throw a legal punch there.

Don't be frightened to be one of a kind.

Waited for too long to jimmy frenemies into a refrain.

No sleep till Berlin. Gonging for a sound healer.

That disposability of a pharmaceutical aesthetic.

You live the life that you want as best you can as
   an American of color.

Gangly poems make me want to run like hell.
I'm mercurial & I'm not going to let that be
  watered down.

What goes on inside a Garage Band.

Got a pandemic puppy— Basil.

Time & Space, you are sublime!

I still feel bad making you be on pointe all the time.

Three sides of equal length.

Best place to take a leak.

I'm just from the riots & my voice is hoarse.

What's the history behind the dead body of the
    little boy

washed up the shore of a Greek Island?

I have rocks to climb.

The leverage of the footprints of cadavers.

It's hard to say with certainty who deserves
    utter desperation.

This is the art of planting a cubicle inside a bud.

Enmeshment isn't quite an alignment.

The stars of remembrance are dark.

Molasses that run through your thoughts.

Which panic has collapsed into the rain?

Both sky & bird in locomotion.

To smash servile writing. Wreck it.

I want to hear about your day trip with
    Caetano Veloso.

On sitting for a portrait by you.

The variants are sneaky bastards.

I'm too horny not to see the word made flesh.

Hakuna matata. Spare me your flag emojis.

What's all this jazz about your being immaculate?

A body can say things that words cannot.

The complete honesty of a truth searcher.

I can't really hide anywhere. I stand out from
   the crowd.
This is what happens whenever I wear my gold gown.
Intangible things are fun to speak about.

You can taste the wastage.

Strive, think it through a bit.

I focus on the music of Scriabin.

It matters whether they love each other or not.

I feel deeply for those who are not saints. They
chime with me.

Rarely do the powerful hold the hands of the
powerless.

It's sometimes difficult to think beyond tragedy
at the keyboards.

I'll keep bearing witness to their crimes against
humanity.

We're the virtues of the minnow. Paradox is
promiscuous.

Inside the helix there is no helix.

Fly to me your deconstructions.

Beneath your blouse your arousal is as sure as
a sunflower.

I'm enjoying the heck out of our continuation.

Mabruk!! You popped my cherry.

The duty of each generation is to horrify the
previous generation.

Perfect for free flying. This vital need to write.

We doin da best we cans.

Beyond the pale? That's where you have the best
of everything.

Seeing the Beatles crossing Abbey Road back then.

The lady rides a crocodile.

Rome's Piazza Vittorio. Paninis. The banana is
your signature.

A shortcut to the end of my shift.

Security tag & funeral procession.

I check if the contents of a wooden drawer are
    still there.
Thistles multiply inside a narrative.
My age comes with bladder issues.
Astronauts blast off. A spotlight hates ambivalence.
Everything we are is in this kiss.
We can't go back to being unwritten in the field
    of play.

❊

Which this time I will not fail to say that I keep run-
ning into the post-plastic tornado. My own part in
browning the best answer. Worry beads back to back
in the stirrups. An untethered country. A simple loving
of cunt-sucking.

Ask about the fugal trip of second chance. In order to
become a star the wheat needs to room with the chaff
for a very long time.

Lest you neglect the feeling of the catfish sitting in that
chair. The wonders of debris and wreckage. Don't let
go of this pied piper. It's as if you use your dance to
tax my icon. Brooding residue, busy plumule. This
time nothing is going to change.

A truer way of being in the black heat of hope. How
far we were from the continual penance of letting a
god sink into God. More or less crying out for more
of your realness.

Chasing a rebirth, the river rang true. We rest our
cheeks on wonder. Excellence of spinal dust. Came
into bloom on a one-man railroad. A throb of the my-
thos.

Tougher than the toughest night. This foreskin is burn-
ing. Granular cellular inquisitor. Dismemberment of
penury. What will it take to actually live our dream? A

perspective shaped by the sweetness of long walks.

Doing the business of mania while my morning becomes a misspelled word.

They want to untie themselves from emptiness. A blast furnace is in the Transcendental. Call it the poetry of the black eye. Goths at Gettysburg. You're unimaginable in a polling booth.

I was there when Molly Bloom said Yes. Where were you? A lot of talk about frozen margaritas. And paradise is still under construction. After all, I was a resident alien not too long ago. Pitying of three Babylons. Diminishment of forever. That nation is a criminal enterprise. Do I have to tell you that my life matters?

This morning exceeds the limits of being on the inside of your outside. To feel things out, to literalize the diaspora. I learned, by kissing, who not to kiss. These are not only the loves that pass through me. A single cup of coffee can romance you all night.

As you grow older you come closer to your own necessary emptiness. There are speed bumps even in love. Are you a flash in the pan or the canary in the coalmine? You go with the brain to take a symptom, a smudge, a pitch. It wants me to draft the small talk of mountains.

And that joy of the return to the body. We fucked in the open with respect for the sacred. There is some-thing positive about keeping karma in motion. Making funny faces at strangers. Throwing our hearts at the screen and throwing the screen at the world. If you buy cultural remix, can I borrow it? Under the threat of hell, what have poets got to lose?

This mindfulness is not frictionless. Unrolling a condom from my soft dick. Your mailbox is full.

So you know: I'm very big on churning. A dream that slipped out of a cream. A dream in thrall to flinty armor. Swayed wildly mid-song. Leave the fascist march. It's uncool to cancel people. The cobble stone streets heave against the wind. Where are we? The dead seem more alive than we are.

The war chased them up the trees where they slept.
Bombing raids over the townships continued. They
hardly ever wondered how to say Peace or God in
Igbo.

In motion towards the silent hour under the tutelage
of stone, totem, star. You broke my bracelet. About
stinging: you're in the clear. You take the two roads
of two hands. When there are more worn-out shoes
than the presence of a man, the climate carries me on
its shoulders.

The buildups, the takedowns, do not disappoint the
sunlamp. She snatched it even though it was nostalgia
in a can. Beachwater, beachwear.

Helio Oiticica samba-danced into his "Penetrables."
If I foot-lick you, will you breast-suck me? Agent
provocateur battered by midnight, by midnight,
by midnight. The rain with pepper. Summer at its
cruelest.

So while birding, hatred and harassment sought you
out and menaced you in Central Park. Fruitage. Foot-
age. Without an acknowledgement of a white matte
page, without an acknowledgement of an open fly,
there's still a poem sitting around if anyone wants
to read it. Not as social cachet, not as sentimental
question that is settled.

Thank you for giving me my first room in the placenta!

Blue boats in my shoulder bag. I have never seen this kind of stained glass before. Softness becomes kindling. The song asks for a marble desk, asks for a way to enter your bodies.

Your hat is on straight, but your head is not. I left nothing to chance save an untucked shirt. The solution to this crisis is inside this crisis. I should have seen the waning libido coming. I've got to dash off things and then go for a bottle of tequila. From the start I never liked the part about a rubble. The slideshow of denigration. The howl inside a riddle.

A curtain exiling itself from itself. A suppler mode of parting. Fragrance of softness. White vinyl of many loves. The nursing nipple of a word. It keeps moving. That beautiful tangent. Illumination in coitus.

Hardly a day goes by now without good cheer. You say: move. I move. I'm inside. I'm inside of you. The light comes down on our genitals and they sparkle. Shades of the color of perfection. This tilt that shows these shoulders are made for kissing. Lines written while falling and rising. The abandon through which love travels.

Juices to rejoice in. Symbiosis of queer ones and unprotected nerds. Unlike a heap of academic footnotes. We concede we adore secretions. But this winter is mouthy. It does matter that this does not matter. The anatomy of quartz shows us how to read a poem in total darkness.

He has salt in his voice. Harbor Bridge: memories temporarily accepted. Tear at saturation point. This nurturing space for the erotic lives of blood oranges. Very blackly. Sheltering kelp, she unmoors her boat. She watches as some poems get their tans. She had met those poems somewhere before. Those knots tied and untied by language. The moss in flight.

I'll fall harder for the bait next time. I run my fingers through my thoughts. In boot camp, betrayal is never banal. You decided to test your theory by wearing a boa constrictor. Some faces, when looked at deeply, can drown you. It's one of the reasons why I know that New York City is a chord.

Your rigorous analysis means nothing to my power of refusal. Democracy is one of the tools we use in sharing danger. Thank you, rain, for cleaning the dog poop on the sidewalk! Four cubic yards of panic gone. Potatoes are heroes. Pass the almonds, she said, with an earnest tone. You don't know what's going on. I know what's going on. I've seen everything. Swam with manatees while sirens got detoured.

As drums rampaged across the interstate, mortars flew. The misguided spirits didn't disappoint us. Shattered lives after shattered lives. Vanquish paralysis. Rinse the river. Help cat sitters sit.

It's pretty swanky to chew loudly near asters. Terms of intrusion. Philosophy twitters in the ghetto. Slippage

is subliminal. You believe there are caresses within a
mathematical equation.

We swing into a piece never played, never heard. To unmake this bed there will be no further hints. Ankles cast off yellow ribbons. The cruise ship knows what the perfect half cookie is all about. This is what I see: on the upper deck she comes tripping. Quicksilver of who you want and who wants you.

I need to remember the name of that metallic darkness. A sentence full of fruit. I'm not sure it's a good idea to hide out on the loudest island. It takes time to draw a line in the sand. Standing beside you, making you a cocktail, and talking about the haunting art of Eva Hesse. Turn around. Push deep. We side with the black radiance of her work.

Middle hinge. I'm on the way to the train otherwise known as the subway. Dark with love, kicking up dust. I was born to long for you. I can't talk about a compass without mentioning the laughing chandelier.

Ready the next grave. There's a growing gap between what they say and what they do about mass shootings. Facing pages, raven beak, red poppy, resolution of owlglasses. A rebound coincident with Mali script. Nuthatches, cardinals aim for the gradation of ochre.

Sex in love or love in sex. A sense of where we are.
Bisection of love in our arms. Doubling back to the
lover humming, to the lover falling up. Draped thighs
on the move won't save the best for the last. All
aboard with anglers; verdant uprooting. The streets
run between our lineages.

Late cubing and overworking of Walter Benjamin's
The Arcades Project/Passagen-Werk. The political gaze
does not disturb birdseeds. Puppets surfing the Web.
A tendency towards citing your status update.

Charlatans and the sexing of destruction. Packrats
and algorithms. If the camera could speak of living
absently. How radical are they when they run from full
presence? Presuppositions or another pill to pop.

Of the automaton you can't obliterate. Father, son
(and Holy Mother?)

A fidelity to the writings of Ulrike Meinhof. You were
there and did swing time since wisdom began to burn
with sage. Their Balaclavas, their mushroom clouds.
To be. To just be. With. No place. To go. And. Just. Be.
Crosshatch. In rotation.

Old layer fowl. Chewing its bones. Star. Guilder.
Premier. Sicilian capers in salt. We don't make love
communicating just with bodies. These pinky nails
of the bivalves. Bloodsided, blindsided, broadsided.

To punctuate with no hard feelings isn't a kind of peace. An expanse of purple in the Black sublime. Hammerhead throbbing in Mars. The subject has gone a few steps more than a single intelligence singing.

Although the garden knows them too well, they're very different from one another in their luck and chaos. A half-eaten lettuce. A half-eaten pear. French horn, instant rapport. A shopping cart shudders. Absence has been lost somewhere along the way. The statuette thirsts for acoustic panels. She came on to me. Came on to me. I was a sailor and sailed around her waist.

The scent of sex is a coronation.

I loved the way you played the guitar the way you made movies the way you made love.

Doors open to let instants scatter. No one rocks a sharp suit like you.

From houseware to warware. Hand me the pliers at the end of the beginning.

How can we bring lovemaking out of the bed and into the garden? The new eyes given to us by travel. This future that is always involved with birdsong. With each touch we realize we're linked to beautiful soil. Linked to the musing cup and scatting bowl. A full-stop and a sentence are yet to patch up their differences. Conundrum is exactly what's needed.

We're not in a hurry to reach our destination.

You chose not to ask for a reason to believe in a life stripped down.

Shipshape, smoke and mirrors.

Tangle of desire and befuddlement.

Above the waterline. Blue skies from hell.

ROOF BOOKS

the best in language since 1976

Recent & Selected Titles

- FOR TRAPPED THINGS by Brian Kim Stefans, 138 pp. $20
- EXCURSIVE by Elizabeth Robinson, 140 pp. $20
- I, BOOMBOX by Robert Glück, 194 pp. $20
- TRUE ACCOUNT OF TALKING TO THE 7 IN SUNNYSIDE
  by Paolo Javier, 192 pp. $20
- THE NIGHT BEFORE THE DAY ON WHICH
  by Jean Day, 118 pp. $20
- MINE ECLOGUE by Jacob Kahn, 104 pp. $20
- SCISSORWORK by Uche Nduka, 150 pp. $20
- THIEF OF HEARTS by Maxwell Owen Clark, 116 pp. $20
- DOG DAY ECONOMY by Ted Rees, 138 pp. $20
- THE NERVE EPISTLE by Sarah Riggs, 110 pp. $20
- QUANUNDRUM: [i will be your many angled thing]
  by Edwin Torres, 128 pp. $20
- FETAL POSITION by Holly Melgard, 110 pp. $20
- DEATH & DISASTER SERIES by Lonely Christopher, 192 pp. $20
- THE COMBUSTION CYCLE by Will Alexander, 614 pp. $25
- URBAN POETRY FROM CHINA editors Huang Fan and
  James Sherry, translation editor Daniel Tay, 412 pp. $25
- BIONIC COMMUNALITY by Brenda Iijima, 150 pp. $20
- QUEENZENGLISH.MP3: POETRY: POETRY, PHILOSOPHY,
  PERFORMATIVITY, Edited by Kyoo Lee, 176 pp. $20
- UNSOLVED MYSTERIES by Marie Buck, 96 pp. $18.95

Roof Books are distributed by
SMALL PRESS DISTRIBUTION
1341 Seventh Street • Berkeley, CA. 94710-1403.
spdbooks.org

Roof Books are published by
Segue Foundation
300 Bowery #2 • New York, NY 10012
seguefoundation.com